On the TV of Life

RICKY CLEMONS

PUBLISHED BY FIEDLI PUBLISHING, INC.

Copyright ©2020, Ricky Clemons
ALL RIGHTS RESERVED.

No part of this publication may be reproduced, stored in a retrieval system, or transmitted in any form or by any means—electronic, mechanical, photo-copy, recording, or any other—except for brief quotation in reviews, without the prior permission of the author or publisher.

ISBN: 978-1-60414-922-7

Published by

Fideli Publishing, Inc.
119 W. Morgan St.
Martinsville, IN 46151
www.FideliPublishing.com

Table of Contents

On the TV of Life 1

The Cock of Our Lives 3

Living Your Dreams 4

In Every Skin Color 5

The Lord Created a Wonderful Thing................................ 7

In a Den of Wolves 8

My Heavenly Father 10

In Your Holy Tabernacle... 11

Appreciate Other People... 12

Back Up What It Talks 13

Whether You Are 14

If I Complain About Anything 15

We Should Not Be Surprised 16

Only The Lord.. 17

God Exists 18

No Control Over.. 19

Is Like a Mystery.. 20

There is a Thin Line Between... 21

We Can't Put Our Trust in Money 22

Believe 24

God Will Never Fall Asleep... 25

I Thank You for Helping Me 26

Silence is a Blessing 27

Performing Miracles today... 28

Real Stories 29

Please the Lord... 30

Living Their Lives 31

It Will Hurt Gods Heart 32

We Go Through Some Things... 33

People Are No Different Today... 34

We Just Have No Idea 35

Believe That It's Alright 36

Being In Good Health.. 37

Come Into and Leave Out 38

You Have Ways Of 39

Before Jesus Christ Comes Back Again 40

For All The World 41

Teach Your Children 42

Life Maybe Only One 43

Your Own Soul Salvation 44

Jesus is the Judge, Lawyer and Jury... 45

The Animals Have Sense Enough 46

Everybody's Lives Matter 47

Way Back Then 48

To the Promised Land	49
Around the Clock	50
In this World	51
Only Jesus Christ	52
Can Always Make A Way	53
Should Not be Surprised	54
We Can Look on the Bright Side	55
Always Need To	56
Where is Our Faith?	57
Sometimes We Have To	58
Busy for Jesus	59
The Invisible God	60
A Witness of Jesus Christ	61
Be So Quick	62
It's Always a Good Thing	63
I was Young and Foolish	64
The Love Language	65
Go out into the Night	66
Must Be Careful About	67
An Experience	68
We Christians Have Jesus Christ	69
Most of the People	70
Jesus Never Sinned	71

Jesus' True Sheep 72

On Guard 73

If We Call Ourselves a Christian 74

I Once was blind 75

Prayers 76

On the TV of Life

You and I are watched every day and every night on the TV of life.

The holy angels are watching our every move.

They're watching what we say, whether they are good words or bad words.

They are watching what we do, whether we are doing good deeds or bad deeds.

The fallen angels are watching you and me to try and tempt us to sin against God.

The TV of life is for the unseen to watch.

You and I are seen in the eyes of the unseen.

The TV of life is for the unseen to watch you and me, who are seen in the eyes of the unseen.

You and I can watch one another, and may not see the real you and me because we can disguise ourselves by wearing a spiritual mask.

The angels in heaven see our true condition.

The fallen angels see our true condition.

Most of all, God in heaven sees our true condition.

You and I can play act with one another, but we can't play act with the angels and God.

The TV we watch in this world can't compare to the TV of life that shows everyone's words and deeds to the angels and, most of all, to God.

God and the angels will not miss out on anything that we say and do in this life.

The TV that we watch can't show us everyone in this world.

What it shows can be fleeting and may never be shown again.

You and I and all of the world will never go off of God's TV screen.

Every living soul is watched by God and the angels, every day and every night.

God is not only watching, but He will also direct our lives if we love and obey Him every day.

The TV of life that we watch has directors for every show.

Those directors are not perfect to direct every TV show and earn a good rating.

On the TV of life, God can only give you and me a good rating.

He knows our motives and intentions to be true or false.

We can't play act with God the father, the Son and the Holy Spirit, or even the heavenly Angels and fallen Angels on the TV of life.

They are watching everything that we say and do.

Our souls are so naked to the unseen on the TV of life.

We can be saved in Jesus Christ, who covers over our naked soul in His precious blood that the unseen can't uncover.

The Cock of Our Lives

We don't want the cock of our lives to crow about us wherever we go.

We need the cock of our lives to crow good things about us, who would be wise to seek and find spiritual things about the Lord Jesus Christ who is the King of Kings.

It's never a good thing to deny Jesus Christ, who the cock will obey and crow in our lives.

if we don't be a witness of Jesus Day after day, the cock of our lives will crow our disloyalty unto the Lord.

Why would we deny Jesus in our works, when the more we give Jesus the glory and praise the more that cock of our lives won't crow.

One of Jesus' disciples named Peter did not acknowledge that he was with Jesus when he was asked the questions about being with Jesus.

Peter denied Jesus three times for the cock to crow to let him know that he was not worth a dime.

The cock of our lives will crow our selfish ways of not being like Jesus is selfless every day.

The cock of our lives will crow our actions if we say one thing and do another, not being like Jesus on any day.

\

Living Your Dreams

Living your dreams is not about getting rich.

For a man can have a job digging down in the ditch and be happy about doing it.

Living your dreams is not about becoming great when you just love your dreams that make you happy.

Living your dreams is not about making a name for yourself.

For in life you can be like a book on a shelf for someone to open and read you to get blessed.

Living your dreams is what you love to do, so don't let anyone take that away from you.

The Lord and Savior Jesus Christ gives us dreams for you and me to bring to the table of life.

Living your dreams will prosper your soul if your dreams are good dreams from the Lord who knows your heart's desires.

You and I have dreams that burn like fire in our hearts.

We want to be what fulfills us, but there is no fulfillment like giving Jesus all of our trust beyond our dreams that will trust Jesus Christ.

The best dreams that we can ever have in our lives is to live our dreams unto the Lord who paid our price on the cross for us to be saved from our sins.

Jesus is the creator of good dreams that have no end in His holy name that we can live our dreams and never be disappointed.

Living your dreams in Jesus Christ is the best dream to live and do spiritual things that won't suppress your dreams.

In Every Skin Color

There are beautiful women in every skin color.

There are strong men in every skin color.

There are intelligent women in every skin color.

There are intelligent men in every skin color.

There are good women in every skin color.

There are good men in every skin color.

There are honest women in every skin color.

There are honest men in every skin color.

There are trustworthy women in every skin color.

There are trustworthy men in every skin color.

There are faithful women in every skin color.

There are faithful men in every skin color.

There are respectful women in every skin color.

There are respectful men in every skin color.

There are educated women in every skin color.

There are educated men in every skin color.

There are tall women in every skin color.

There are tall men in every skin color.

There are short women in every skin color.

There are short men in every skin color.

There are big women in every skin color.

There are big men in every skin color.

There are bad women in every skin color.

There are bad men in every skin color.

There are talkative women in every skin color.

There are talkative men in every skin color.

There are quiet women in every skin color.

There are quiet men in every skin color.

There are great women in every skin color.

There are great men in every skin color.

God loves everybody in every skin color.

God loves little children and he loves teenagers in every skin color.

We all are God's beautiful rainbow colors of people who the devil hates in every skin color.

Racism is of the devil who hates the human race.

There are brave women in every skin color.

There are brave men in every skin color.

There are funny women in every skin color.

There are funny men in every skin color.

There are deceptive women in every skin color.

There are deceptive men in every skin color.

There are working women in every skin color.

There are working men in every skin color.

There are lazy women in every skin color.

There are lazy men in every skin color.

There are proud women in every skin color.

There are proud men in every skin color.

The devil hates every skin color.

He knows that every skin color will enter into heaven one day when Jesus Christ comes back again.

Every skin color of people will be saved in Jesus Christ and go to heaven where that racist devil was kicked out of forever and ever.

The Lord Created a Wonderful Thing

The Lord created a wonderful thing when he created a father to oversee the protection of his children.

It's a wonderful thing that a father is a provider for all of his children as he will divide equally among his children.

It's a wonderful thing that a father is a counselor to all of his children leading them on the right path in life through the good times and the hard times.

It's a wonderful thing that a father is a good friend to his children to talk to him and trust him to the end.

The Lord created a wonderful thing when he created a father to navigate all of His children through this unpredictable and untrustworthy world where a father will take a wrist to save his children's lives from harm and danger.

A Christian father will always teach his children to love and obey the Lord who created a wonderful thing in every way when he created a father to teach his children how to pray.

A man can make a baby but it takes a father to raise his children to give God all the glory and praise.

A man can make a baby, but it takes a father to correct his children to do right under the great blue Sky.

A man can make a baby, but it takes a father to love his children regardless of the mistakes that they make.

Lord created a wonderful thing when he created a father to be like a battery charger to charge up his children to believe in Jesus Christ and be saved to receive eternal life.

In a Den of Wolves

When I was young and in the military.

I was like a sheep thrown in a den of Wolves.

I joined the army at the age of eighteen.

I was immature and inexperienced to the real world that I saw in the military.

That real world was a den of Wolves because of some bad influences that I got caught up in.

I was young and wanted to be a soldier in the army to represent my country.

I didn't know that I would be influenced to use drugs in the military.

The pressure was on me because a lot of the soldiers were using drugs and drinking alcohol and smoking.

I was like a sheep in a den of Wolves that probably didn't know that they were going to tear me up.

Out of my own ignorance I use illegal drugs and caused myself to get sick so I got discharged from the army.

It hurt my heart that my military career was over, as if I had never joined the army.

I know today thanks to the Lord that my life was spared.

The Lord wanted to spare my health but He gave me a free will to choose right from wrong.

I knew that it was wrong to use those drugs but I used them anyway.

I knew I had to hide from my commanding officers when I was Under the influence of drugs.

I was the Lords sheep in a den of Wolves.

I was his lost sheep and did not know it.

The Lord kept the Wolves from taking my life that I had taken too lightly.

It's a miracle to me that the Lord brought me as far as I have come, to know that He has saved me from those Wolves.

There were other young soldiers like me in that den of Wolves.

Hopefully today they are saved in Jesus Christ who knows how to shut the Wolves' mouths.

My Heavenly Father

My real blood father was never in my life.

I can feel the pain when I watch a movie on the TV that a father leaves his children.

I can feel the void of an absent father even today in my middle age.

It's so important for a father to be in his children's lives especially if he is a good man.

Too many fathers are not in their children's lives and leave them feeling void.

I had so longed for my father to be in my life as a little boy.

When I was a teenager I went out searching to find my father.

When I found Him, I found a big part of myself.

Before my father died I was at peace with him and with myself to know that I understood myself when I got to know my father.

I have a heavenly Father who makes me spiritually whole.

My heavenly Father has never left me or forsaken me.

God has always been in my life and been there for me.

God is a father who will never leave me alone in this sinful world where earthly fathers can fail to be in their children's lives.

In Your Holy Tabernacle

There is no better place to be in other than Your holy Tabernacle O Lord.

My Lord and savior Jesus Christ, Your holy Tabernacle is the best place that I ever been in.

I have been on top of a mountain that is not like being in your holy Tabernacle.

I've been in airplanes, and that is not like being in Your holy Tabernacle oh Lord.

I have been in a helicopter, but that is not like being in Your holy Tabernacle, my Lord Jesus.

I have been in a tractor trailer truck and I've been on ships, but neither of those things are like being in Your holy Tabernacle, O Lord.

I've been on some islands, but that is not like being in Your holy Tabernacle oh Lord.

I've been in amusement parks, and that is not like being in Your holy Tabernacle my Lord.

I've been on a nature walk that is not like being in your holy Tabernacle, O Lord Jesus Christ.

I've been in movie theaters that are not like being in on Your holy Tabernacle, my Lord.

Your holy Tabernacle, my Lord, is where I love to be on Your holy Sabbath day of rest.

It is the most remarkable and peaceful place on earth to be in.

O Lord, Your holy Tabernacle is pretty much safe to be in to worship You.

Appreciate Other People

Can you ever imagine if there were a world full of people exactly like you?

They would have the same bad habits like you.

They would have the same bad ways like you.

They would say the same words like you.

They would think the same thoughts like you.

They would do the same things like you.

They would act the same way like you who won't like that.

It would make you miserable to see that day after day.

Even a proud person who was hung up on himself or herself would not like to see a world full of people being exactly like him or her.

I am not saying to not love yourself.

It's good to love yourself, but it's also good to love other people for who they are.

God created us all to be different.

Even identical twins are not exactly alike.

They each have their own personality.

It's always good for you and me to appreciate other people for who they are, with their own personality.

If everyone in the church was exactly alike and had the same spiritual gifts, we would be so confused and miserable.

God didn't make a mistake when He create us so different.

Back Up What It Talks

Money can't always back up what it talks.

Jesus can always back up what He talks in His holy word.

Material things can't always back up what they talk.

Jesus can always back up what He talks in spiritual things.

Our enemies can't always back up what they talk.

Jesus can always back up what He talks because Jesus will always walk the walk.

This world can't always back up what it talks.

Jesus can always back up what He talks because Jesus overcame the world.

Jesus Christ, our Lord, created talk and He knows how to always talk to you and me who don't always listen to Him.

When Jesus talks to you and me, He will always back it up with the first and last words to say.

Whether You Are

Whether you are a Christian or not a Christian, you will have some good days and bad days.

If you are a Christian, you will know that Jesus will be there for you and not against you day after day.

Whether you are a Christian or not a Christian, you will go through some bad things in this life.

If you are a Christian, you will know that Jesus will give you the strength to go through the bad things in this life.

Whether you are a Christian or not a Christian, you will have some enemies.

If you are a Christian, you will know that Jesus can make your enemies make peace with you.

Whether you are a Christian or not a Christian, you will die one day.

If you are a Christian, you will know that you are saved in Jesus Christ, who will give you eternal life when He comes back again.

If I Complain About Anything

If I complain about anything, I disrespect the Lord, who gives me all that I need.

Many people can't see, but they won't complain.

Many people can't hear, but they won't complain.

Many people can't walk, but they won't complain.

Many people don't have any food to eat, and they won't complain.

Many people don't have clean water to drink, and they won't complain.

Many people are homeless, and they won't complain.

If I complain about anything, I insult the Lord, who will supply all of my needs.

Many people are sick, but they won't complain.

Many people are dying, but they won't complain.

Many people can't talk, but they won't complain.

Many people don't have a job, but they won't complain.

Many people don't have anything. but they won't complain.

If I complain about anything, I dishonor the Lord, who brought me this far when He didn't have to do it.

If I complain about anything, I push away the Lord, who won't push me away from Him when I need Him to be there for me all the time.

We Should Not Be Surprised

If we have a woman president one day, we should not be surprised.

If we have another earthquake in our nation, we should not be surprised.

If we get another deadly virus, we should not be surprised.

If we get another mass shooting one day, we should not be surprised.

if we have another protest in this nation, we should not be surprised.

If we have more killings by racist policemen, we should not be surprised.

If we have more wildfires, we should not be surprised.

If we have more hurricanes, we should not be surprised.

If we have more tornadoes, we should not be surprised.

If we have more floods, we should not be surprised.

If we have more child abuse, we should not be surprised.

If we have more people turn their backs on the Lord, we should not be surprised.

If more people are lost in their sins, we should not be surprised.

We Christian should not be surprised about anything in this world.

We Christian should not be surprised about Jesus Christ coming back again one day.

Only The Lord

Only the Lord can always protect us from evil.

Many people will live their lives like evil doesn't exist in this world.

Many people will live their lives like evil can't come their way.

Many people will live their lives like evil can't do any harm or be a danger to them.

Evil is a real, true presence all around you and me, day after day.

You and I can't protect ourselves from evil that can come our way on any day.

Evil would kill us dead if we had no protection from the Lord.

Evil can be invisible, like a deadly virus that we can't see.

Evil is of the devil, who is evil all the time.

He hates what is good, and God is good all the time.

Evil will want to kill us dead whether we're being mature or immature.

Evil will want to kill us dead whether we're being good or bad.

Evil will want to kill us dead whethr we're being educated or not educated.

Only the Lord can always protect you and me from evil.

Evil will want to kill us dead whether we're rich or poor.

Evil will want to kill us dead whether we're well or sick.

Evil will want to kill us dead whether we are white, black, brown, or yellow.

Evil will want to kill us dead whether we're young, middle aged, or old.

Evil shows no respect to people.

Only the Lord can always protect you and me from evil.

God Exists

When people live through a terrible accident, God exists.

When soldiers live through a war, God exists.

When people live through the coronavirus, God exists.

When people live through a mass shooting, God exists.

When people live through an earthquake, God exists.

When people live through a hurricane, God exists.

When people live through a tornado, God exists.

When people lived through a flood, God exists.

When people live through cancer, God exists.

When people live through a wildfire, God exists.

When people live through their bad Choices, God exists.

All who are still alive today are because, God exists.

Life is from God every day, and God's son, Jesus Christ, is the life.

God will exist forever and ever.

God existed before he created the heavens in the earth.

When we live to see another day, God exists.

No Control Over

We don't like things that we have no control over.

It makes us feel weak and makes us feel like we will break into pieces.

We don't like things that we have no control over.

It makes us feel helpless like a boat that has a big hole in it while it's out in the ocean.

We don't like things that we have no control over.

It makes us feel lost, like going to vote and losing the election of the candidate we voted for.

We don't like things that we have no control over.

It makes us feel like an alcoholic who can't stay sober even for one day.

We don't like things that we don't have control over.

It makes us feel like we are in a boxing ring and we know we're going to lose.

Jesus Christ, our Lord, has control over all things.

Nothing will happen unless He allows it to happen, according to His holy word.

Jesus has control over all things every day so that the devil can't do more to us than what Jesus Christ allows him to do.

This makes us so blessed, even though we have no control over many things in this world.

Is Like a Mystery

The free will choice is like a mystery.

We don't know who will choose to tell a lie.

We don't know who will choose to steal something from someone.

The free will choice is like a mystery that is hard to solve.

We don't know who will choose to take his or her own life.

We don't know who will choose to kill someone.

We don't know who will choose to be jealous of someone.

The free will choice is like a mystery that can leave us without a clue.

We don't know who will choose to come back to Jesus Christ before it's too late.

We don't know who will choose to put their trust in Jesus Christ.

We don't know who will choose to turn their backs on Jesus Christ.

The free will choice is like a mystery that we can't figure out.

We don't know who will choose to believe in Jesus Christ and be saved.

We don't know who will choose to reject and deny Jesus Christ.

There is a Thin Line Between

There is a thin line between right and wrong in this world.

It's easy to say and do something wrong in this sinful world.

Up in heaven everything is right all the time.

There is a thin line between perfection and making a mistake.

It's easy to make a mistake, and it's hard to strive for perfection in this sinful world.

Up in heaven, perfection is everywhere all the time.

There is a thin line between good and evil in this sinful world.

It's easy to speak evil and do evil things in this sinful world.

Up in heaven, good is forever present.

There is a thin line between being saved and being lost in this sinful world.

Up in heaven is where the saved will go when Jesus Christ comes back again.

Only Jesus can save souls from being lost in sin.

There is a thin line between our free will and our destiny in this sinful world.

It's easy to make our destiny in hell.

Up in heaven is the destiny of all who believe in Jesus with the free will choice.

There is a thin line between you and me in this sinful world.

It's easy for you and me to judge one another.

Up in heaven, God is the only judge to judge our life here on earth.

We Can't Put Our Trust in Money

We can't put our trust in money.

Money can let us down.

Money can run out.

Money can deceive us.

We can't put our trust in money.

Money can disappoint us.

Money can stress us out.

Money can make us mean.

We can't put our trust in money.

Money can make us proud.

Money can make us jealous.

Money can make us sick.

We can't put our trust in money.

Money can make us greedy.

Money can make us not content.

Money can make us selfish.

We can't put our trust in money.

Money can make us materialistic.

Money can make us hasty.

Money can make us violent.

We can't put our trust in money.

We can put our trust in Jesus Christ, who will never run out of power.

Money can run out of power.

We can put our trust in Jesus Christ who owns everything.

Money can run out and lose everything.

We can't put our trust and money that can fall short.

Jesus Christ, our Lord and Savior, will never fall short of anything.

We can't put our trust in money.

Money can get us into debt.

Jesus Christ will never get us in debt.

Believe

Everybody wants somebody to believe what they are telling them.

Nobody wants to be told they are a liar.

Even a liar wants people to believe what he or she says.

Everybody wants to be believed by what they say.

You and me want people to believe what we tell them.

It makes you and me feel good when people we know believe what we tell them.

It surely pleases the Lord Jesus Christ when we believe in him that should be every day.

If we can believe what people say then we can truly believe what Jesus says In his holy word.

His word is everlasting truth that we can always believe.

We can't imagine how it makes Jesus feel when we believe what he tells us through his Holy Spirit.

Even a little child wants you and me to believe what he or she tells us.

To believe what someone tells us is very effective to our mind.

To be believed by other people is very powerful no matter if we tell them the truth or a lie.

God Will Never Fall Asleep

God will never fall asleep on you and me who need to sleep away into the deep unconscious.

God watches you and me all day long and all night long, and he sees our rights and wrongs.

God will never fall asleep on you and me when we go through the storms of life that God always sees.

God will never fall asleep on you and me who fall asleep on God when we have no clue about what is going on in this world.

God will always stay awake to see what we do right and see the mistakes that we make.

God needs no sleep at all when we need to sleep no matter if we are great or small.

God will never fall spiritually asleep on you and me who can fall spiritually asleep on God and go into the deep darkness of sin.

The devil loves for you and me to be spiritually asleep.

He is like a hungry Wolf attacking a lost sheep that would be you and me if we fall spiritually asleep on God.

God will never fall asleep on you and me who can keep our faith in God's son Jesus Christ who is one with God in truth and grace.

I Thank You for Helping Me

Oh Lord, I thank you for helping me to survive in this life.

Oh Lord, I thank you for helping me to cope in this life.

Oh Lord, I thank you for helping me to cherish this life.

Oh Lord, I thank you for helping me to live this life.

Without your help, oh Lord, I would be better off never being born in this life.

Without your help, oh Lord, my life would be a mess.

Without your help, oh Lord, my life would be worthless.

Oh Lord, I thank you for helping me to enjoy this life.

Oh Lord, I thank you for helping me to be real in this life.

Oh Lord I thank you for helping me to be good in this life.

Without your help, oh Lord, I would be lost in this life.

Without your help, oh Lord, I would be miserable in this life.

Without your help, oh Lord, I would be nothing in this life.

Oh Lord, I thank you for helping me to be content in this life.

Oh Lord, I thank you for helping me to love and obey you in this life.

Silence is a Blessing

When it is silent, the Lord can speak to you and me so clear.

The Lord can really tell you and me what we need to know so that we know what is going on.

Silence is a blessing from the Lord, who kept silent at some times when His enemies asked him some questions.

When it is silent, the Lord can show us what we need to see.

When it is noisy, it is hard to hear the voice of the Lord.

The Lord loves to dwell in silent places.

Silence can surely show us the truth about things going on in our lives.

Silence is a gift from the Lord for you and me to use day after day.

Silence is like good medicine to take to get well.

We can rest our minds when it is silent.

We can get a good night's sleep when it is silent.

We can think clearly when it is silent.

Silence can help us to make the right choices.

Silence can help us to wise up.

Silence is a blessing from the Lord who can speak to you and me so good when it is silent.

Performing Miracles today

When Jesus Christ was living on earth, he performed many miracles before many people.

Many people believe that Jesus was the Messiah and the Son of God.

Many people believe that Jesus had healed them.

Many people believe that Jesus had cast demons out of them.

Many people have no doubt that Jesus was sent to them from God in heaven.

Many miracles do happen today, but many people don't give Jesus the glory and praise for them.

Many people will say that it was luck that spared their lives from death.

Many people will live through a terrible car accident and won't thank Jesus for showing mercy on them and sparing their life.

Jesus is the same Jesus today like he was thousands of years ago when he lived on earth.

It is by no chance that we are still alive today after going through some terrible things.

It's a miracle that we are still alive, and that miracle is from the Lord Jesus Christ.

If Jesus allowed the devil to always have his way, we would all be dead — both good and bad people.

Jesus is still performing miracles today in our lives.

We need to give Him all the glory and praise when we come out of a terrible ordeal in our lives.

Real Stories

The Bible has real stories about real people who had real problems in their lives.

Those real stories in the Bible can blow our minds and make us feel like we were there.

The Bible has many stories that we can learn from.

Real stories can surely have a good or bad effect on us.

It depends on what the story is about to cause us to feel something.

The real stories in the Bible can change our lives for the better if we take them to heart.

The best stories are told in the Bible, where every story is so very true.

All of the stories in the Bible are about giving God the glory and praise and to acknowledge that God is above and beyond all things.

If you want to read a good story that will move your heart, then read the stories in the Bible that have no lies in them.

The Bible has good stories in it that you can read to your children and learn some good things in life.

The Bible stories are real for you and me to apply in our everyday lives.

The best story is Jesus Christ talking to many people and healing them, and then giving up his life to save us from our sins.

Please the Lord

It's much better to please the Lord, who will never let us down.

If we try to please man, he can let us down.

It's much better to please the Lord, rather than trying to please man, who can be so displeased with you and me.

It's much better to please the Lord, who will never deceive us.

Man can deceive us in many ways each and every day.

It's much better to please the Lord, who will never change on us.

If we try to please man, he can change on us.

It's much better to please the Lord, rather than trying to please man, who can turn his back against you and me.

The Lord will never turn his back against you and me for pleasing Him.

Pleasing the Lord Jesus Christ will give us joy and peace.

Trying to please man can cause us to feel bad.

Living Their Lives

Many people are living their lives saying what they want to say, and they don't care about how anyone else feels, day after day.

Many people are living their lives doing what they want to do, and don't care about who is influenced by their actions.

Many people are looking and searching for real, true fulfillment in this world.

They believe that by doing their own thing they will find fulfillment in their lives.

Many people are finding out that the real, true fulfillment is only from the Lord Jesus Christ, who fills every Christian's life with love, joy and peace.

Many people are living their lives like a wild beast, and don't care about who they disrespect under the great blue sky.

Many people will not seek to find Jesus Christ in His holy word that will never change for anyone in this life here on earth where fulfillment is very low under the sign of the rainbow.

Many people are living their lives like the wind that can blow in different directions.

Only the Lord knows how their lives will end in this world that can't fulfill anyone's life.

It Will Hurt Gods Heart

It will hurt God's heart if we hurt our pets.

The animals mean so much to God; He loves them and created them for His pleasure.

It will hurt God's heart if we hurt one another; God loves us more than the animals.

We should love one another so that we don't hurt anyone's heart.

God created you and me in his image.

God didn't create the animals in his image, but he still loves the animals so very much.

God loves us much more than he loves the animals, but God will never treat them bad.

We should never hurt our pets or any animal that belongs to God.

There are people who love to hurt other people for no good reason.

There is never a good reason to hurt someone's heart, especially on purpose.

No one should ever take any pleasure in hurting anyone.

No one should ever take any pleasure in hurting an animal.

A dog can love us more than a human being, who God will never hurt.

You and I can hurt God's heart if we don't love and obey Him.

We Go Through Some Things

Sometimes we go through things that we just don't understand for a long time upon this sinful land.

Sometimes we go through things that we will never forget, and things may not look so clear.

Sometimes we go through some things that can stress you and me.

Sometimes we go through some things that will make us feel emotionally weak and take our minds to a dark place.

Sometimes we go through some unexpected things that are hard to face up to, no matter where we live at.

Sometimes we go through some things that will catch us off guard; what we don't see coming is hard to swallow.

Whatever that we go through, we can pray to Jesus Christ and trust Him to make things right in our lives.

People Are No Different Today

People are no different today than the people who were here thousands of years ago.

Today, many people are good like they were thousands of years ago.

Today, many people are wicked like they were thousands of years ago.

Today, many people are geniuses, just like the people who were geniuses thousands of years ago.

Today, many people are intelligent, like people who were intelligent thousands of years ago.

Today, many people are scientists, just like the scientists of the past.

Today, many people are moral like the people who were moral thousands of years ago.

Today, many people are immoral like people were immoral thousands of years ago. Jesus Christ is no different today than He was thousands of years ago when He lived on earth without sin.

Jesus Christ is the same yesterday, today, and tomorrow — He will never change.

We Just Have No Idea

We just have no idea about how the Lord can bless us if we put all of our trust in Him.

We just have no idea about how the Lord can open a door for us, who should love our Lord Jesus Christ more and more.

We just have no idea about what the Lord can do for us, when we don't see what the Lord sees in you and me.

We just have no idea that the Lord is making a way for us who should never doubt what Jesus Christ can do for you and me.

We just have no idea about how far the Lord will take us in life, regardless of the mistakes we make.

We just have no idea about how the Lord will use us in this sinful world where many people's love has blown out like a fuse.

We just have no idea what the Lord will do for us next.

We can get nothing good without the Lord's approval, and many people take that out of context because they don't obey God's golden rules.

Believe That It's Alright

A lot of people weren't raised up in the church.

They believe that it's all right to lie.

They believe that it's all right to have sex outside of marriage.

They believe that it's all right to curse.

They believe that it's all right to drink alcohol.

A lot of people weren't raised up in the church.

They believe that it's all right to smoke cigarettes.

They believe that it's all right to fuss and fight.

Some people who are raised in the church believe that it's all right to live in adultery.

They believe that it's all right to abuse their spouses and children.

No sin is all right with Jesus Christ, who died on the cross to save us from our sins.

Doing wrong things is not all right with Jesus, who does everything right all the time.

A lot of people believe that it's all right to break God's commandments and think they will still be saved if they are living in sin.

Being In Good Health

Being in good health is worth more than all the money in this world.

Being in good health is truly a blessing from the Lord.

So many people are in bad health and wish that they were in good health.

When you have your mind and physical strength, nothing else in this world can top that.

When you have good health, you have everything to prosper in good living.

It's a terrible thing to waste your mind away with drugs, alcohol and other bad things.

Many people are wearing their bodies down by working too much and even exercising too much.

When you are in good health, the Lord can use you much more.

You can't do anything much for the Lord if your health is bad.

Good mental health and good physical health go together.

One is not much good without the other.

If you are in good health, you can do many things.

Without good health, your talents and skills are like sand running out of an hourglass.

Come Into and Leave Out

People can come into and leave out of your life.

Jesus Christ will come in and stay in your life, if you want Him to.

Loved ones can come into and leave out to the grave, which is a permanent way out of your life.

It can hurt our hearts especially when loved ones come into our lives and leave out of our lives through separation or divorce, or just moving away to live in another state or country.

It can even hurt for a dog to come into and leave out of your life.

Jesus will never come into and leave out of our lives.

When he comes in, He will stay in our lives as long as we don't turn our backs on Him.

It's never a good thing for loved ones to come into and leave out of our lives, like we never existed to them.

So many children's hearts have been broken by a father or mother who left them.

Even many spouses have had their hearts broken by their husband or wife leaving them.

Coming into people's lives and leaving out of people's lives is only a small thing to some people, but it's a moral thing to want to hold onto loved ones so they never leave.

When Jesus comes into our lives, He wants us to stay with him and to hold onto him for as long as we live.

Jesus loves to come into our lives, and He loves to stay in our lives.

The choice is ours to keep Jesus in our lives.

You Have Ways Of

O Lord, You have ways of bringing a backslider back to You at the right time.

O Lord, You have ways of bringing someone near to you after their faith has been tested.

O Lord, You have ways of reaching out to a lost soul who has no intentions of getting to know You.

O Lord, You have ways of using someone to help someone else call on Your holy name.

O Lord, You have ways of opening up someone's eyes to see the truth to set him or her free from the lies.

O Lord and Savior Jesus Christ, You have ways of giving someone a second chance to believe in You and be saved.

O Lord, You have ways of saving a soul from being lost in sin.

Before Jesus Christ Comes Back Again

No one dies and goes to heaven before Jesus Christ comes back again to raise the righteous dead.

We will go to the grave and stay there until Jesus Christ comes back again.

If people went to heaven after they died, then Jesus Christ wouldn't have to come back to raise the righteous dead.

When people die, they know nothing; they can't see anything; they can't talk.

Only the living can do these things every day.

Jesus is the resurrection — no one else.

Everybody will not go to heaven.

Only the righteous who are saved in Jesus Christ will go to heaven.

There are fallen angels who can appear to be someone who is dead.

Fallen angels can even talk to you and sound like a person you've lost to death.

Jesus Christ is the only truth in this life.

Jesus won't deceive you and cause you to believe that you can talk to your dead loved ones.

The devil is all about deceiving us so we believe that lie.

The devil has the power to appear to be a dead loved one, making it seem like he or she can talk to us and is looking down on us from heaven.

No one dies and goes to heaven before Jesus Christ comes back again.

Only Jesus has the power to raise the righteous dead and change the righteous living from mortal to immortality.

For All The World

Sermons about Jesus Christ are for all the world below the heavenly gates of everlasting pearls.

Bible school lessons about Jesus Christ are for all the world to learn about Jesus, who will always stand strong and stern on His holy word.

Songs about Jesus Christ are for all the world, where sin will pull us down like crabs in a barrel.

Poems about Jesus Christ are for all the world that needs Jesus.

His mercy rains down upon every man, woman, boy and girl.

Our righteous living about Jesus Christ is for all the world to see Jesus living in our lives.

Our righteous talk about Jesus Christ is for all the world to hear about the price that Jesus paid on the cross for the sins of all the world.

God's son, Jesus Christ, is for all the world.

He wants to save all the world, even those who don't believe in Jesus Christ, who is no fake.

Teach Your Children

If you teach your children about Jesus Christ, you will teach them about the highest moral living in this life.

If you teach your children about Jesus Christ, you will teach them righteous living the opposite from any strife.

Teach your children about Jesus Christ, who gave up His life to pay the price for them to be saved in God's amazing grace.

There is no other better teaching than to teach your children about Jesus Christ, who loves to also reach out to children to believe in Him and love and obey Him.

Teach your children about Jesus Christ, the light of the world that's never shining dim day after day and night after night.

If you teach your children about Jesus Christ, you will never regret knowing that Jesus Christ is always so nice.

To bless your children with spiritual things beyond material things that can never wear away.

Life Maybe Only One

Life may be only one second away from death for someone.

Life may be only one minute away from death for someone.

Life may be only one hour away from death for someone.

Life may be only one day away from death for someone.

Life maybe only one week away from death for someone.

Life may be only one month away from death for someone.

Life may be only one year away from death for someone.

Only the Lord truly knows how long that we will live.

Only the Lord can truly add more years to our lives.

Only the Lord will always see death coming our way.

Only the Lord can truly hold back death from us another second, minute, hour, day, week, month, or year.

Life may be only one inch away from death for someone.

Life maybe only one yard away from death for someone.

Life is not eternal in you and me, who were born in sin to one day die.

Life is eternal in Jesus Christ our Lord.

Your Own Soul Salvation

You must work out your own soul's salvation.

You must believe in Jesus Christ for yourself.

You can't believe in Jesus Christ for anyone else.

You must work out your own soul's salvation.

You must love and obey Jesus Christ for yourself.

You can't love and obey Jesus Christ for someone else.

You must work out your own salvation.

You must have faith in Jesus Christ for yourself.

You can't have faith in Jesus Christ for anyone else.

You must work out your own soul's salvation.

You must put your trust in Jesus Christ for yourself.

You can't put your trust in Jesus Christ for anyone else.

You must work out your own soul's salvation.

You must have hope in Jesus Christ for yourself.

You can't have hope in Jesus Christ for anyone else.

You can't pick up your cross and follow Jesus Christ for anyone else.

You must pick up your cross and follow Jesus Christ for yourself.

Jesus is the Judge, Lawyer and Jury

A lawyer wants to win his or her case according to the truth that he or she presents to the judge who will rule the verdict.

The judge loves to hear the truth if he or she is a fair judge.

A lawyer has to prove to the judge that he or she is truly representing their client and they are telling the truth.

No lawyer wants to lose his or her court case whether they prove or not prove to the judge that their client is innocent of a crime.

Jesus Christ, our Lord and Savior, is our judge, lawyer, and jury in the courtroom of heaven.

We all are judged by the Lord for every good and bad thing that we do.

We all are judged by the Lord for every good word and bad word that we say.

We all are judged by the Lord for every good thought and bad thought that we think.

Jesus Christ, our Lord, will win every case that He represents.

If you and I are saved in Jesus, He will represent our case when it gets to the courtroom of heaven.

Jesus is a judge who is always fair.

Jesus is a lawyer who is always right.

Jesus is a jury who is never prejudiced.

Jesus will never lose a case.

The Animals Have Sense Enough

When there's thunder and lightning, the animals have enough sense to keep quiet until the storm is over.

When there's thunder and lightning in our lives, we may be noisy about complaining instead of keeping quiet and waiting on the Lord to pass the storm out of our lives.

The animals will fear storms in their lives.

We know that lightning can strike our houses if we have loud music playing during the storm.

We know that lightning can strike our houses if we have our TV on.

We know that lightning can strike our houses if we are noisy during the storm.

It makes good sense to keep quiet during the storm.

The animals have enough sense to go somewhere and hide from the storm, but we may not go and hide the storms in our lives by finding the Lord.

There is always safety in the Lord, who can calm the storms.

We need to use our God-given good sense to put all of our trust in Jesus Christ, who the thunder and lightning will obey and cease from you and me.

The animals have enough sense to know when there is a storm.

You and I can walk into a storm and not have enough sense to take cover in the Lord.

Everybody's Lives Matter

Everybody's lives matter to the Lord Jesus Christ, who is always greatly concerned about everybody's lives.

The Lord shows respect for people who treat everybody equally in every way each and every day.

No one is better than anyone else in the Lord's eyesight.

The Lord will see if we're living right or living wrong in his eyesight.

Everybody's lives matter all the same to the Lord, who will never avoid giving justice to everybody.

All lives matter to God in heaven above this old sinful world where many lives are shoved away from equality because of the color of their skin.

Through Adam and Eve, we all are human beings in this world that is populated with men, women, boys and girls whose lives matter to Jesus Christ every day and every night under the sun, stars and moonlight.

Way Back Then

Way back then, in my childhood years, God blessed my mental and physical health so dear.

Way back in my teenage years, God kept me strong as I was going through some changes in life that weren't a wrong thing for me to go through.

Way back then, in my young adult years, God watched over me as I made some bad choices that God didn't allow to kill me, who is so glad to be here today and know that God loves me.

Way back then, in my past years, God had a purpose for me to make the devil so mad about seeing me believing in Jesus Christ, who is the Son of God, being in my life.

He always wanted to be in my life if I chose Him to be in my life, but way back then I was living a lie.

To the Promised Land

Jesus has promised us that He will come back again to take us to the promised land in heaven one day.

We children of God today are like the children of God who were slaves in Egypt waiting on God to deliver us.

Jesus Christ, our Lord, is our deliverer today.

He will come back from heaven with power and glory to deliver us from the Egypt of this world, to the promised land you and I will go to one day, for holding on to Jesus Christ as we go through our trials that last only for a moment.

This whole world is a slave and only Jesus can set us free, if we confess and repent of our sins unto him.

It was Jesus who spoke to Moses in the burning bush up on Mount Sinai.

Jesus is our deliverer, who came into this world in the fullness of time that he was needed the most to fulfill His heavenly Father's holy will.

One day, Jesus will deliver you and me, and all of His righteous children, from this old sinful world and take us to heaven's promised land like He says in His holy word.

When we get to heaven. we will see Moses and all of the Hebrews who didn't disobey God in the wilderness.

Around the Clock

We need to love and obey the Lord around the clock.

Jesus Christ, our Lord loves, us even though we are not always on time to yield to the Holy Ghost.

Jesus is always on time around the clock to supply all of our needs on cold, warm, cool and hot days that we need Jesus in every way.

Around the clock is no time to Jesus Christ, for whom time doesn't exist throughout His eternal life.

Around the clock is our time here on earth, where our time is too short to not put Jesus first and above everyone and everything in our lives.

You and I can lose track of time and it can get away from us.

We can't put our trust in time around the clock, because we must put our trust in Jesus Christ who time will always trust and obey.

We are stuck with the time around the clock, when God's time can knock our time out of time to be mocked.

In this World

We live in a world where many people will let you talk and say what you want to say without listening to you.

They are not going to change their ways, regardless of what you say to them.

Many people already have their minds made up about what they want to do, whether it's fair or not fair to me and you.

This world has many people who just don't care to say and do what is right, because they fear rejection and have no clue what Jesus Christ can work out for them.

Jesus Christ created this world and He knows what it takes for anyone's life to change for the better and improvement in this world.

This is no Christian's home, where sin has pulled many people down like crabs in a barrel.

Every day, many people are moving so fast in this world, heading toward a life living in the flesh, when Jesus is the best one to head towards on the west, east, north and South sides of this world.

Only Jesus Christ

Only Jesus Christ was perfect without sin when he lived on earth among sinful men.

I know that I am not perfect without sin; I was born in sin and must confess and repent until my life ends.

I have said some wrong words to shove some people away from me.

I have done some wrong things that seemed to be right in my eyesight.

Since I have been living in this world, I have never seen a perfect human being under the sun and full white moonlight.

Only Jesus Christ was perfect without sin.

Jesus Christ was born of the Holy Ghost and a virgin mother in His life on earth.

God created Adam and Eve perfect without sin, but they both chose to sin against God when they lived in the Garden of Eden.

Because of Adam and Eve's sins, all of mankind is born in sin.

Only Jesus Christ was perfect without sin when he lived on earth among sinners to set all men free from living in sin that He will destroy in the end.

Can Always Make A Way

Only the Lord can always make a way for us to escape from pride that will take us to a fall.

Only the Lord can always make a way for us to escape from trouble that we can never trust.

Only the Lord can always make a way for us to escape from fear that can overcome us and make us so stressed out.

Only the Lord can always make a way for us to escape from lies so we can run into the truth of God's holy word.

Only the Lord can always make a way for us to escape from evil that can even come to us in a dream that has some effect on our lives.

Only the Lord can always make a way for us to escape from our selfishness if we pray to Him and repent of our sins before we lay down to sleep.

Should Not be Surprised

We Christians should not be surprised about what will happen next under the great blue sky.

We Christians should know that we are living in the last days now and that this world will get worse and worse in every way.

We Christians should not be surprised that more and more bad things will happen because the devil's time is short on earth.

We Christians know that God's word is being fulfilled in these last days of perilous times that are moving so fierce across the land.

We Christians will be saved in Jesus Christ, our Lord, who is still on the right-hand side of God on His holy throne.

Jesus will one day come back again and take us to our heavenly home, and we Christians should not be surprised about that.

We Christians should not ever be surprised, without a doubt, that this world will get no better, because the devil is running to and fro through the earth to cause as many as he can to be lost in sin, no matter what level of education people have in this sinful land.

We Can Look on the Bright Side

We can look on the bright side, and put our hope in Jesus Christ who is not a hoax.

We can look on the bright side, knowing that we can put our faith in Jesus Christ who walked on the water full of grace.

We can look on the bright side, and we can put our trust in Jesus Christ who died on the cross for all of us.

We can look on the bright side, where we can love and obey Jesus Christ who is coming back again for us one day.

We can look on the bright side, knowing that we have free will to deny ourselves, pick up our cross and follow Jesus up on the hills and down in the valleys of our lives.

We can look on the bright side, and we can confess and repent of our sins unto Jesus Christ who can clean up the messes we make in our lives.

We can look on the bright side, knowing that we can be saved in Jesus Christ, who can give us eternal life.

We can look on the bright side and give Jesus Christ all the glory and praise that Jesus deserves in the winter, spring, summer and fall.

Always Need To

We always need to love the Lord.

We always need to obey the Lord.

We always need to read the bible.

We always need to know more about the Lord.

We will always need to have more faith in the Lord.

We will always need to trust the Lord.

We will always need to keep our hope in the Lord.

We will always need to confess our sins to the Lord.

We will always need to repent of our sins to the Lord.

We will always need to love our neighbors.

We will always need to hold onto the Lord.

We will always need to keep our eyes on the Lord.

We will always need to give what belongs to the Lord.

We will always need to deny ourselves and pick up our cross to follow the Lord.

We will always need to pray unto the Lord.

We will always need to live right unto the Lord.

Where is Our Faith?

Where is our faith in Jesus when things are not going right?

Where is our faith in Jesus when trouble comes our way?

Where is our faith in Jesus when we are sick?

Where is our faith in Jesus when we have problems?

It's so easy to have faith in Jesus when things are going well.

It's easy to have faith in Jesus if we have no trouble.

It's easy to have faith in Jesus when we are well.

It's easy to have faith in Jesus when we have no problems.

Where is our faith in Jesus if our prayer is not answered?

Where is our faith in Jesus if our life is in danger?

Where is our faith in Jesus when we don't see our way through our trials?

Where is our faith in Jesus when we don't know what to do?

We have our faith in Jesus, and it is only for Jesus to judge.

Jesus will always judge our lives so very fair.

Sometimes We Have To

Sometimes we have to look back onto the past to see where we are at today for us to be glad that the Lord brought us through the past.

Sometimes we have to look back into the past in order to see the future that has the Lord's presence to come around under the sun, moon and stars.

sometimes we have to look back into the past because there is nothing new under the sun here and there and everywhere.

Sometimes we have to look back into the past to understand what is going on today that is also in the Lord's hand.

In this sinful world many things will happen over and over again for only the Lord to know what to do until the world ends.

Sometimes we have to look back into the past to see the Lord Jesus Christ being there for us in setting us free from the things that could have killed you and me.

Busy for Jesus

We should be busy for Jesus, like the sunlight is busy shining its beautiful rays so bright.

We should be busy for Jesus, like the full, white moonlight is busy glowing all night.

We should be busy for Jesus, like the stars that are busy sparkling so high up above in the sky far from the ground.

We should be busy for Jesus, like the wind is busy blowing here and there to the end of the earth.

We should be busy for Jesus.

The Invisible God

The invisible God is the God who answers prayers.

The invisible God is the God who lives beyond the ozone layers.

The invisible God is the God who created all things.

The invisible God is the God we never seen.

Many people will make seen things their god.

The holy angels know doing that is odd.

The seen things have no power, unlike the invisible God who is all-powerful and makes good things happen to me and you.

The invisible God is all around us for you and me to give Him all of our trust.

Only the Son of God, who is Jesus Christ, sees the invisible God throughout His eternal life.

The angels cannot look upon the invisible God.

Only Jesus is worthy to look upon Him, because Jesus Christ is Lord and is equal with the invisible God who will give us our reward in heaven one day.

A Witness of Jesus Christ

Producing songs in Jesus name is a witness of Jesus Christ.

Writing poems in Jesus name is a witness of Jesus Christ.

Helping people in Jesus name is a witness of Jesus Christ.

Preaching sermons in Jesus name is a witness of Jesus Christ.

Teaching Bible lessons in Jesus name is a witness of Jesus Christ.

Talking about Jesus is a witness of Jesus Christ.

Praying to Jesus is a witness of Jesus Christ.

Going to church in Jesus' name is a witness of Jesus Christ.

Loving people in Jesus' name is a witness of Jesus Christ.

Living right in Jesus' name is a witness of Jesus Christ.

Giving Jesus the glory and praise is a witness of Jesus Christ.

Having faith in Jesus is a witness of Jesus Christ.

Waiting on Jesus to work things out is a witness of Jesus Christ.

Putting trust in Jesus is a witness of Jesus Christ.

Being saved in Jesus is a witness of Jesus Christ.

Confessing and repenting of our sins unto Jesus is a witness of Jesus Christ.

Forgiving people in Jesus' name is a witness of Jesus Christ.

Telling others about Jesus is a witness of Jesus Christ.

Be So Quick

We can sometimes be so quick to tell someone what is right and what is wrong, without taking the time to listen to what he or she has to say.

We can be so quick to run people away from us, because of talking too much — even about the Lord.

We can sometimes be so quick to judge people for what they say and for what they do.

We can sometimes be so quick to form opinions of people without the facts about what caused them to say something wrong and do something wrong.

Jesus wasn't always so quick to prove that the Pharisees were so wrong about him.

We can sometimes be so quick to want to be right about what we say and only see our own way of being right when we may be so wrong.

We can sometimes be so quick to want to tell people off about themselves and tell them all about how wrong what they say and do.

If Jesus was so quick to withdraw His Holy Spirit away from the world, we wouldn't have a chance to be saved in Him who is so patient with us all.

It's Always a Good Thing

Everything we see is not always good to see.

Some things we don't need to see.

Everything we hear is not always good to hear.

Some things we don't need to hear.

Everything we feel is not always a good thing to feel.

Some things we don't need to feel.

Everything that we say is not always good to say.

Some things we don't need to say.

Everything we think is not always good to think.

Some things we don't need to think.

Everything we touch is not always good to touch.

Some things we don't need to touch.

Everything we eat is not always good to eat.

Some things we don't need to eat.

Everything we do is not always good to do.

Some things we don't need To do.

It's always a good thing to see God's handiwork.

It's always a good thing to hear the word of God.

It's always a good thing to feel the power of the Holy Ghost.

It's always a good thing to think on the Lord.

It's always a good thing to do the will of the Lord.

I was Young and Foolish

I was young and foolish and didn't know the Lord Jesus Christ, who was so good to me in my young life.

I was young and foolish and didn't know the ways of truth in my life , but Jesus knew me in my young days.

If I had been a Christian then like I am a Christian today, I would not have made so many mistakes.

I am so happy that the Lord didn't let me die in my sins when I was young and foolish.

When I was young and foolish, I did more wrong than right and didn't really know that Jesus' almighty hand was holding me together to see this day in the land of the living.

If I had been a Christian in my young years, I would have made a lot of good choices being in God's holy will.

I was young and foolish, but the Lord gave me a second chance to love Him and keep His commandments so that I could advance in His spiritual things that are eternal beyond my mortal life.

The Love Language

People will pretty much understand the love language every day, as even a child will know if he or she is loved.

Even a dog will know if he is loved, because an animal will show some love in return if the animal receives love.

Love is a language that everyone can speak in so many ways.

A normal person won't reject love on any day.

The love language is God's language to all the world, where the great and small need to be loved.

The love language is from heaven above, where God is love forever and ever beyond this world.

Many people have fallen out of love with God and have lost their love language with Him.

The love language is a language for every race, creed and color of people to speak, especially by our actions where love or hate can be truly seen every day.

Go out into the Night

Thieves will usually go out into the night to steal.

Murderers will usually go out into the night to kill.

Adulterers will usually go out into the night to cheat on their spouses.

A rat will usually go out into the night to enter into a house.

Judas went out into the night to betray Jesus Christ.

Party people usually go out into the night to party all night long.

Jesus went out into the night to pray all night long without a doubt.

Today, going out into the night is not a good thing to do — a lot of people have lost their lives in the night.

The astronomers will go out into the night to explore the stars and planets that God created so very far from this world.

Must Be Careful About

We Christians must be careful about what we say and how we say it each and every day.

We Christians must be careful about the company we keep and have coming in and out of our houses.

We Christians must be careful about where we go, here and there in the rain and snow.

We Christians must be careful about what we watch on the TV screen where every show is not good to watch.

We Christians must be careful about how we dress, whether we are lean or fat.

We Christians must be careful about what we do and be careful about what we listen to.

We Christians are supposed to represent Jesus Christ who has changed our lives through the price He paid for our sins.

We Christians must be careful about what we eat and drink, so that others will see our good example sooner or later.

We Christians are supposed to love and obey Jesus Christ while we live under the sunlight rays.

We Christians must be careful about what we do to our neighbors and not to beat them up with the truth of God's holy word always being good spiritual food to eat every day.

An Experience

It Is hard to talk about what we haven't experienced.

It is hard to sing about what we haven't experienced.

It's hard to write about what we haven't experienced.

An experience with Jesus Christ is to know that He answered our prayers.

An experience with Jesus Christ is to be baptized and submerged underwater.

An experience with Jesus Christ is to confess and repent of our sins to Him.

An experience with Jesus Christ is to be born again in the Holy Spirit of God.

An experience with Jesus Christ is to love Him and keep His commandments.

Many people will talk about Jesus Christ but they have no experience with Jesus.

Many people will sing about Jesus Christ but they have no experience with Jesus.

Many people will write about Jesus but they have no experience with Jesus.

An experience with Jesus Christ will be going through some trials for His holy sake.

We Christians Have Jesus Christ

Doors have a lock.

Houses have a foundation.

Trains have a horn.

We Christians have Jesus Christ.

Dogs have a bark.

Lions have a roar.

Kangaroos have a jump.

We Christians have Jesus Christ.

Bikes have pedals.

Radios have signals.

Televisions have antennas.

We Christians have Jesus Christ.

Ships have a steer.

Birds have wings.

Apples have seeds.

We Christians have Jesus Christ.

Most of the People

Most of the people back in the Bible days didn't believe that Jesus was the way, truth and life.

Most of the people back in the Bible days didn't believe that Jesus was the Son of God who laid down His life on the cross to save us from our sins.

Most of the people in these last days don't believe in Jesus Christ, who is the Savior of the world.

Only a few people will walk through the gates of pearls, compared to so many people who will be lost in their sins.

Only a few people will be on the right course to pick up their crosses and follow Jesus Christ to the end of the world.

Only a few people truly love Jesus Christ, who most people will shove away from their lives.

Most of the people in this world will reject Jesus to the end of their lives, and will still believe that they will make it into heaven when they die.

Jesus Never Sinned

Jesus never sinned, not even one time, when he lived on earth under the sunshine.

Jesus was tempted in every way, but he did not sin against God on any day.

We can call on the name of Jesus Christ and He will give us power in our lives to resist the devil's temptations and strife.

Jesus never sinned, not even one time.

Jesus knew the devil was not worth a dime, and he's still not worth a dime today under the sunshine.

Jesus became sin on the cross, where He died to save us from our sins under the sky.

Jesus rose from the grave with the victory over our sins to save us all, even though Jesus never sinned.

Jesus' True Sheep

Jesus' true sheep will hear His voice in His holy word, which will keep you and me on the spiritual course.

Jesus' true sheep will obey His voice in His holy word, which will let us know if we are saved or lost.

Jesus' true sheep will deny self and pick up their crosses to follow Jesus, who paid our cost.

Jesus' true sheep will love Jesus with all of their hearts on the good days and bad days that are not so distance apart.

You and I will know if we are Jesus' true sheep, if we stay spiritually awake and are never spiritually asleep.

You and I will know if we are Jesus' true sheep, if we live right by Jesus' holy word that is spiritual every day and every night.

We will know if we are Jesus' true sheep, if we love Him and obey His commandments every day we are in the land of the living.

On Guard

We need to ask Jesus to help us be on guard against the devil's schemes that can knock us down real hard in sin.

We need to ask Jesus to help us stay on guard against the devil's devices that can poison our hearts with sin.

We must be on guard at all times against the devil who has human agents who can look so divine but will try to deceive you and me.

Being on guard against the devil is always a good thing, because the devil will try to fool you with his brown grass that looks green.

We need to always be on guard through our ups and downs in life.

We need to always live unto our Lord Jesus Christ, who was always on guard against the devil who is right now full of evil and trying to corrupt our lives.

If We Call Ourselves a Christian

If we call ourselves a Christian, we can't be telling lies that Jesus Christ never told when He lived on earth.

If we call ourselves a Christian, we can't be greedy for worldly gain like unsaved people of the world who don't care about causing anyone some pain to get their worldly gain.

We Christians must live right by the Lord every day, knowing that Jesus is the way, truth and life like the Bible says.

If we call ourselves a Christian, we can't compromise with the devil who can disguise himself as an angel of light to deceive you and me.

We Christians must pray to the Lord asking for help to see the devil's scheming and crooked ways each and every day.

If we call ourselves a Christian, we won't say foolish words and do foolish things that are not like Jesus Christ.

We Christians must ask Jesus to help us live a renewed life.

I Once was blind

I once was blind to the truth, but now I see the truth in God's holy word.

I know that Jesus Christ is the root of the truth that I see today.

I once was blind to the light of the world, but today I can see that Jesus Christ is the light of the world, shining His glorious rays through my mind and heart.

I once was blind to love, but today I can see love in Jesus Christ, who is the love of God.

The price that Jesus paid for my sins is nothing but pure love that the angels sing about in heaven above this sinful world.

I once was blind, but now I see.

I am no longer blind spiritually, for I can see the spiritual things looking so divine through Jesus Christ, my Lord and Savior.

Jesus is spiritual day after day so that I can see good things happening when I pray to my Lord.

Prayers

The Lord will answer a lot of our prayers that the Holy Spirit takes up through the ozone layers.

We are so blessed that the Lord won't avoid answering a lot of our prayers.

When our prayers are answered, we know it is extraordinary in this sinful world below the heavens.

The Lord is always on time to answer our prayers, but we may sometimes think that the Lord doesn't care to hear from us.

When prayer goes up, the devil falls down off his high horse with a big frown on his face.

Prayers are our lifeline to the Lord Jesus Christ, and the devil can't break that line during the day or the night.

www.ingramcontent.com/pod-product-compliance
Lightning Source LLC
Chambersburg PA
CBHW050042080526
44586CB00014B/1419